# THE
# JUICE
# BOOK

# THE JUICE BOOK

## Over 100 recipes for healthy juicing

## Syd Pemberton

PENGUIN BOOKS

PENGUIN BOOKS

Published by the Penguin Group
Penguin Group (Australia)
250 Camberwell Road, Camberwell, Victoria 3124, Australia
(a division of Pearson Australia Group Pty Ltd)
Penguin Group (USA) Inc.
375 Hudson Street, New York, New York 10014, USA
Penguin Group (Canada)
90 Eglinton Avenue East, Suite 700, Toronto ON M4P 2Y3, Canada
(a division of Pearson Penguin Canada Inc.)
Penguin Books Ltd
80 Strand, London WC2R 0RL, England
Penguin Ireland
25 St Stephen's Green, Dublin 2, Ireland
(a division of Penguin Books Ltd)
Penguin Books India Pvt Ltd
11 Community Centre, Panchsheel Park, New Delhi – 110 017, India
Penguin Group (NZ)
Cnr Airborne and Rosedale Roads, Albany, Auckland, New Zealand
(a division of Pearson New Zealand Ltd)
Penguin Books (South Africa) (Pty) Ltd
24 Sturdee Avenue, Rosebank, Johannesburg 2196, South Africa

Penguin Books Ltd, Registered Offices: 80 Strand, London, WC2R 0RL, England

First published by Penguin Group (Australia), a division of Pearson Australia Group Pty Ltd, 2005

10 9 8 7 6 5 4 3 2 1

Design by Jay Ryves © Penguin Group (Australia)
Illustrations by Jay Ryves
Cover photographs by Georgie Cole
Penguin Books would like to thank Sunbeam, Bodun and Wheel and Barrow,
for kindly lending their merchandise for the photography shoot.
Typeset in Bauer Bodoni by Post Pre-press Group, Brisbane, Queensland
Printed and bound in Australia by McPherson's Printing Group, Maryborough, Victoria

National Library of Australia
Cataloguing-in-Publication data:

Pemberton, Syd.
   The juice book: over 100 recipes for healthy juicing
   Includes index.
   ISBN 0 14 300360 7.
   1. Fruit juices. 2. Vegetable juices. I. Title.

541.875

www.penguin.com.au

# CONTENTS

# Introduction

Delicious, healthy and natural – what could be better than that?
Well, add simple, no-fuss and affordable and you're almost there.
Juices and smoothies are an easy way to pack a wide variety of fresh
fruit and vegetables, as well as dairy ingredients, into one glass.

These healthy drinks can kick-start your day, or give you an
energy boost midmorning or during that particularly low-energy
period around midafternoon. Also, depending on their ingredients
and how much you consume, they can provide an energy fix that is
low in kilojoules, making them perfect before and after exercise.

Much has been written about the health benefits of raw juicing
as a way of boosting our nutrient intake. Our health guidelines say
that we should consume each day at least two servings of fruit and
five servings of vegetables. Juice can be an easy way to increase your
intake and the variety of fruit and vegetables you consume.

All juices should be consumed as soon as they are made, because as soon as air gets to the juice it begins to oxidise, and vitamins and minerals start to be lost (the juice might also sour).

When putting together the recipes for this book I was amazed by the number of additional therapeutic health benefits that juices and smoothies can provide, such as water intake. An important nutritional fact that we all know but don't all act on is that each of us should consume at least 8–10 glasses of fluids every day. As many fruits and vegetables have a very high water content, juicing is a great way of taking in extra liquid, but with the added bonus of nutrients.

Starting the day with a refreshing raw fruit and vegetable juice or smoothie is much better for you than a breakfast consisting of coffee or tea and a muffin; you'll really notice the difference. Because they are, so delicious, it can be easy to overdo it. If you are trying to keep your weight down, why not dilute the juice with filtered water or sparking mineral water? This is a particularly good idea with some of the strongly flavoured juices.

Not all combinations of fruits and vegetables will appeal to everyone, but the beauty of juicing is that you can experiment to your stomach's content. What may sound like an odd combination can be so delicious that it soon becomes your favourite juice of the month!

# Equipment

Juicing and blending are, in themselves, very simple processes, and the equipment needed really comes down to how often you will be using it. If you are serious about juicing every day, then invest in a juicer with a powerful motor. Similarly, for regular smoothie making, a good-quality blender or food processor is a must.

## Electric juice extractors

As their name suggests, these machines extract the juice from fruit and vegetables. Cut-up or whole vegetables or fruit are fed through a shoot onto a rotating blade that filters the juice into a container, but removes the fibre into a separate container. There are many extractors on the market, and when choosing one to suit your needs it may be helpful to consider the following.

- How easy is it to clean?
- How powerful is the motor?
- What level of extraction is the machine capable of?

Note: add the fibre to a compost heap or worm farm. Or use it to cook with: fibre from carrot, celery and apple can be used in soups, stocks and casseroles and added to simple cake or muffin recipes.

## Citrus squeezers

These can be manual or electric.

Manual citrus juicers are simple to use and easy to clean. They come in varying materials and sizes, and it is a good idea to choose one that takes all sizes of citrus fruit. A wooden reamer is particularly efficient at extracting juice, but it can be messy and is best used over a bowl covered with a nylon sieve to catch any flesh or pips.

Almost all food processors are multi-functional, and many can be transformed into an electric juicer with a simple attachment. The juice is squeezed from the fruit by the rotation of the juicer, and the pips and most of the flesh are caught in a sieve, allowing the juice to run into the bowl below. Most of these electric juicers can handle all sizes of citrus fruit and they are easy to clean.

## Food processors, blenders and hand-held blenders

These electric machines are very good for blending drinks, such as smoothies, where the fruit is soft and a liquid is added to blend the drink. The ones with more powerful motors can crush ice as well as blend food and liquid. Check the manufacturer's instructions before adding whole ice cubes.

The only real difference between food processors and blenders is that food processors do not blend ingredients to a completely smooth purée, whereas blenders and hand-held blenders have this capability.

## Other useful equipment

- small, stiff brush for cleaning fruit and vegetables
- vegetable peeler
- chopping board
- serrated-edge fruit knife
- small paring knife
- spoon for scraping out seeds
- mortar and pestle
- metric cup measures
- metric scales

- sieve
- spatula
- ice-cube trays
- ice-cream scoop
- serving jug
- glasses – cocktail, shot and tall sundae glasses
- long-handled teaspoons
- straws
- swizzle sticks
- airtight containers for 'boost' ingredients (such as linseed meal, glucosamine powder and lecithin)
- brush for cleaning machine

# Ingredients

## Sourcing

Choosing fresh, ripe and seasonal ingredients is essential to making a delicious and healthy juice. Purchase the best-quality ingredients that you can, and only buy from a source that you trust.

A cheap bucket-load of bruised fruit may seem a bargain, but if the fruit (or vegetable) is damaged it may have lost vitamins and minerals and mould may have entered through broken skin. It might not taste that great, either.

Ripe fruit is at its prime, both in terms of flavour and nutrition; from this moment on the sugars begin to break down and the ingredient very quickly loses its nutritional value. It is therefore important to store the produce correctly. In many cases refrigeration will slow down or stop the rate of the cells breaking down, thereby slowing the loss of nutrients and retaining flavour.

Buy organic ingredients if available. The practice of organic farming is based on growing food without artificial pesticides or fertilisers. Companion planting assists in keeping a balance of nutrients in the soil and fewer organic fertilisers are needed for plant growth. Also, certain plants can attract insects that act as predators on other insects, keeping use of organic insecticides to a minimum. For example, planting garlic will act as a general pest deterrent and planting marigolds will deter snails. Organically grown food does not contain artificial pesticides, hormones, growth stimulants or antibiotics, or have waxes or finishes added. It has not been genetically modified or irradiated. Most supermarkets and greengrocers sell some organic produce these days; look for labels saying certified organic.

Alternatively, have a go at growing your own ingredients if you have the space and time. It is amazing how a small, sunny courtyard or balcony can be turned into a seasonal source of food, and there is nothing more satisfying than picking and using your own fruit, vegetables or herbs. A lemon or lime tree grows well in a large pot; many vegetables will be fine in small or large pots; and herbs will be happy on a sunny windowsill.

## Washing

Unless the ingredient is to be peeled, washing the skin before juicing is very important (even if the produce is organic) to ensure that any dirt or residual fertiliser or pesticide is removed. A gentle scrub with a small, soft scrubbing brush will give you the best results.

## Storing and refrigerating

Here are some useful tips on fresh produce, including where and how to store an ingredient, how long it will keep for (both in or out of the refrigerator), and how best to ripen firm fruit.

**Apples** – store in the refrigerator; chilled apples will maintain their crispness for 1 month

**Apricots** – allow to ripen at room temperature, then store in an airtight container in the refrigerator for up to 3–4 days

**Asparagus** – stand spears upright in a jug with their stalks in a little water; cover loosely with a plastic bag

**Avocados** – firm fruit will ripen in 2–5 days at room temperature; to speed up the process, store in a paper bag with a banana for up to 1–2 days

**Bananas** – allow fruit to ripen at room temperature; if buying several, select bananas at different stages of ripeness to ensure they all don't ripen at once

**Beetroots** – leave the tops on and store in the refrigerator in a plastic bag or the crisper for up to 3–4 days

**Blueberries** – remove from the punnet and place in a single layer in a shallow container lined with kitchen paper, then cover and refrigerate for up to 5 days

**Cabbages** – store in a plastic bag in the refrigerator

**Capsicums** – store in the refrigerator in a plastic bag or the crisper for up to 4–5 days

**Celery** – store unwashed in an airtight container or in the refrigerator in a plastic bag for up to 2–3 days

**Cherries** – store in the refrigerator in a plastic bag for up to 5 days

**Cucumbers** – store in the refrigerator in a plastic bag or the crisper for up to 3 days

**Fennel** – store unwashed in the refrigerator in a plastic bag for up to 5–7 days

**Grapefruit** – *see* oranges

**Grapes** – store unwashed in the refrigerator in an airtight container or plastic bag

**Guavas** (pink and white) – allow firm fruit to ripen at room temperature (2–3 days), then store in the refrigerator for up to 2–3 days

**Herbs** – stand herbs in a jug with their stalks in a little water, cover loosely with a plastic bag and store in the refrigerator for up to 4–5 days, changing the water if necessary

**Honeydew melons** – these do not ripen further after harvesting; store at room temperature if whole, or covered in the refrigerator for up to 3–4 days if cut

**Kiwifruit** – allow firm fruit to ripen at room temperature, then store in the refrigerator for up to 2–3 days

**Lemons** – *see* oranges

**Lettuces** – store whole lettuces in the refrigerator in a plastic bag or the crisper for up to 3–4 days, washing and drying leaves as needed. Loose lettuce leaves and other salad leaves (baby spinach, rocket, mescalun, etc), should be washed, dried and placed in an airtight container that does not crowd the leaves

**Lychees** – these do not ripen further after harvesting; store in the refrigerator in a plastic bag for up to 7 days

**Mangoes** – allow to ripen at room temperature, then store in the refrigerator in a plastic bag or the crisper for up to 3–4 days

**Mulberries** – *see* strawberries

**Nashi pears** – store in the refrigerator for up to 2 weeks

**Nectarines** – allow firm fruit to ripen at room temperature, then store in the refrigerator in an airtight container for up to 2–3 days

**Oranges** – store at room temperature for up to 2 weeks; to extend storage life, refrigerate

**Passionfruit** – store at room temperature for up to 10 days; to extend storage life, refrigerate

**Pawpaws** – allow to ripen at room temperature out of direct sunlight, then refrigerate for up to 2–3 days

**Peaches** – allow firm fruit to ripen at room temperature (ripe fruit has a rich yellow colour at the stem end), then store in the refrigerator in a plastic bag for up to 2–3 days

**Pears** – allow firm fruit to ripen at room temperature, then refrigerate for up to 2–3 days

**Pineapples** – these do not ripen further after harvesting; store in a cool place if whole, or store covered in the refrigerator for up to 2–3 days if cut

**Plums** – allow firm fruit to ripen at room temperature, then store in the refrigerator in the crisper for up to 1–2 days

**Rambutans** – store in the refrigerator in a plastic bag for up to 5 days

**Raspberries** – remove from the punnet and place in single layer in a shallow container lined with kitchen paper, then cover and refrigerate for up to 1–2 days

**Rockmelons** (cantaloupes) – these do not ripen after harvesting; store at room temperature if whole, or covered in the refrigerator for up to 3–4 days if cut

**Spinach** – trim and discard stalk ends, then store unwashed in the refrigerator in a plastic bag for up to 3 days

**Strawberries** – remove from the punnet and place in a single layer in a shallow container lined with kitchen paper, then cover and refrigerate for up to 2–3 days

**Tomatoes** – allow to ripen at room temperature, then store in the refrigerator for up to 3–4 days

**Watercress** – stand in a bowl filled with water, cover with a plastic bag and store in the refrigerator for up to 1–2 days

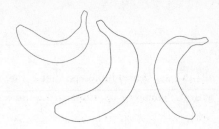

# Nutrition

Vitamins and minerals are essential for our health and wellbeing. They work with the macronutrients, such as oxygen, water, protein, carbohydrates and fat, to enable us to create and use energy and regulate cell function – in essence, to allow the constant growth and repair of our bodies.

Despite them being critical to life, by and large vitamins and minerals cannot be manufactured by our bodies and we therefore need to obtain them from the food we eat. Different foods contain different nutrients, and the fruit and vegetable component of our diet contributes about 1 per cent fat, 7 per cent protein, 10 per cent calories, 20 per cent niacin, thiamine and iron, 25 per cent magnesium, 35 per cent vitamin $B_6$, 50 per cent vitamin A and 90 per cent vitamin C, with the remaining nutrients coming from the other four food groups – dairy, proteins, cereals, and fats and oils. A varied and balanced diet is therefore essential to provide you with the range of vitamins and minerals your body needs.

## Vitamins

Vitamins are essential for health and growth. They are different from, say, fats, proteins and carbohydrates because they are not broken down to give us energy – they help regulate the chemical functions that create and use (metabolise) energy. Vitamins play a vital role in our health and their basic functions are listed opposite.

Our intake of vitamins must be in regular, small amounts. If you keep the body topped up with the right amount of vitamins it will run well; too much at one time may not necessarily increase overall health and vitality and in some cases could have detrimental effects. It is only in cases of poor diets that 'extra' vitamins may be a bonus to health, and the key for people with a normal diet is to have a regular, moderate intake of vitamins and minerals to help the body function optimally.

There are thirteen vitamins essential for good health: vitamins A (and betacarotene), C, D, E, K, plus eight arms of the vitamin B complex – thiamin ($B_1$), riboflavin ($B_2$), niacin ($B_3$), pyridoxine ($B_6$), cyanocobalamin ($B_{12}$), folate, pantothenic acid and biotin.

## Basic functions of vitamins

**vitamin A and betacarotene** – important for maintenance and function of vision, immune system, and hormone-producing glands; antioxidant

**vitamin B** – this range works to metabolise carbohydrates, fats and protein; important for maintenance of hair, skin, nerves, blood cells, immune system, hormone-producing glands and digestive system

**vitamin C** – antioxidant; needed for healthy immune system, hormones, cardiovascular system, nervous system; maintains collagen; aids wound healing

**vitamin D** – regulates absorption of calcium and phosphorus; important for bone and teeth development; assists immune and nervous systems, and hormone system

**vitamin E** – antioxidant; protector for cells against free radical damage; controls blood cholesterol; aids hormone system

**vitamin K** – important for blood clotting; assists calcium metabolism, growth, kidney function, and carbohydrate metabolism

## Minerals

Minerals, like vitamins, are essential to our health and wellbeing. Among their important functions, they ensure growth and are involved in the chemical processes that release energy and synthesise protein. There are approximately twenty minerals known to be necessary for the maintenance and regulation of the functions of the body. The major ones are calcium, iron, phosphorus, potassium, sodium, chlorine, magnesium and sulphur. Trace minerals such as chromium, copper, iodine, manganese, selenium, silicon and zinc are also important to overall health.

### Basic functions of minerals

**calcium** – promotes healthy bones and teeth; needed for muscle and nerve function; helps with blood pressure regulation and clotting; prevents osteoporosis

**chromium** – involved in sugar and fat metabolism; helps cardiovascular system

**copper** – important to immune and nervous systems and joints and bones, and in general metabolism and red cell blood formation

**potassium, sodium and chlorine** (the electrolytes) – essential for maintaining fluid and acid–alkali balance; help regulate nerve and muscle function, and with energy production

**magnesium** – allows metabolism of protein for energy production; interacts with calcium in nerve and muscle function

**phosphorus** – important for metabolism, bones and teeth health, and energy production

**selenium** – antioxidant; assists immune function and hormone production

**silicon** – important for healthy skin and hair, blood vessels and cartilage

**zinc** – involved in metabolism; aids immunity, hormone production and the brain and nervous system; assists in growth and health of teeth and bones, skin, liver

# Nutrition tables

Fruits

| Fruit | Vitamins | Minerals |
|-------|----------|----------|
| Apple | C | potassium |
| Apricot | A, B, C | phosphorus, potassium |
| Avocado | A, B, C | iron, magnesium, phosphorus, potassium |
| Banana | B, C | magnesium, phosphorus, potassium |
| Blackberry | C, E | calcium, magnesium, phosphorus, potassium |
| Blackcurrant | C, E | calcium, phosphorus |
| Blueberry | C | calcium, magnesium, potassium |
| Cherry | A, B, C | potassium |
| Fig | B | calcium, magnesium, potassium |
| Grape white | B | phosphorus, potassium |
| Grape black | B | phosphorus, potassium |
| Grapefruit | B, C | potassium |
| Guava | A, C | potassium |

| Fruit | Vitamins | Minerals |
| --- | --- | --- |
| Honeydew melon | B, C | potassium, sodium |
| Lemon | C | calcium, phosphorus, potassium |
| Loganberry | C | calcium, magnesium, phosphorus, potassium |
| Lychee | C | potassium |
| Mango | A, C | potassium |
| Mulberry | C | calcium, phosphorus, potassium |
| Nectarine | A, B, C | phosphorus, potassium |
| Orange | C | calcium, potassium |
| Pawpaw | C | potassium |
| Passionfruit | C | phosphorus, potassium |
| Peach | A, B | potassium |
| Pear | B | potassium |
| Persimmon | A, C | potassium |

| Fruit | Vitamins | Minerals |
| --- | --- | --- |
| Pineapple | C | potassium |
| Plum | B | potassium |
| Pomegranate | C | potassium |
| Raspberry | B, C, E | calcium, magnesium, phosphorus, potassium |
| Rockmelon (cantaloupe) | A, B, C | magnesium, phosphorus, potassium |
| Strawberry | B, C | calcium, phosphorus, potassium |
| Tangerine | B, C | calcium, potassium |
| Watermelon | A, B, C | potassium |

**Vegetables**

| Vegetable | Vitamins | Minerals |
|---|---|---|
| Asparagus | B, C, E, betacarotene, folic acid | calcium, iron, magnesium, phosphorus, potassium |
| Beetroot and tops | B, C, betacarotene, folic acid | calcium, chlorine, chromium, iron, magnesium, manganese, phosphorus, potassium, sodium |
| Broccoli | C | calcium, iron, magnesium, phosphorous, potassium, sodium |
| Cabbage | B, C, betacarotene, folic acid | chlorine, calcium, iodine, potassium, sulphur |
| Capsicum | B, C, betacarotene, folic acid | calcium, iron, magnesium, phosphorus, potassium, silica |
| Carrot | B, C, D, E, K, betacarotene | calcium, chlorine, chromium, iodine, iron, magnesium, phosphorus, potassium, silica, sodium, sulphur |
| Celery | B, C | calcium, iron, magnesium, phosphorus, potassium, sodium, sulphur |

| Vegetable | Vitamins | Minerals |
| --- | --- | --- |
| Chilli peppers | C, E, betacarotene, folic acid | magnesium, potassium, selenium, sodium |
| Coriander leaves and stalks | B, C, folic acid | magnesium, potassium, sodium |
| Cucumber | B, C, betacarotene | calcium, chlorine, magnesium manganese, phosphorus, potassium, silica, sodium, sulphur |
| Dandelion | B, G, betacarotene, folic acid | calcium, iron, magnesium, potassium, sodium |
| Fennel | B, C, betacarotene | calcium, chromium, cobalt, iron, magnesium, manganese, phosphorus, potassium, selenium, silicon, sodium, zinc |
| Garlic | B, C | calcium, chromium, iron, magnesium, phosphorus, potassium, selenium |
| Ginger root | C | calcium, copper, iron, magnesium, phosphorus, potassium, sodium, zinc |
| Horseradish | B, C | calcium, phosphorus, potassium, sulphur |

| Vegetable | Vitamins | Minerals |
| --- | --- | --- |
| Lettuce | B, C, folic acid | calcium, iodine, iron, magnesium, phosphorus, potassium, silica, sulphur |
| Onion | A, B, C | calcium, iron, magnesium, phosphorus, potassium, sodium |
| Parsley | B, C, folic acid | calcium, chlorophyll, copper, iron, manganese, phosphorus, potassium, sodium |
| Radish and leaves | B, C, betacarotene, folic acid | calcium, chlorine, iodine, iron, magnesium, phosphorus, potassium, silica, sodium |
| Spinach | B, C, K, betacarotene, choline, folic acid, inositol | calcium, iodine, iron, phosphorus, potassium, sulphur |
| Tomato | B, C, K, carotenes | calcium, iodine, iron, phosphorus, potassium |
| Watercress | B, E, C, betacarotene, folic acid | calcium, chlorine, iodine, iron, magnesium, phosphorus, potassium, sodium, sulphur |
| Wheatgrass | B, C, E, K, betacarotene, folic acid | calcium, chlorophyll, cobalt, phosphorus, potassium, sodium, sulphur, zinc |

# Handy Hints and Tips

To make crushed ice, place ice cubes into two plastic bags and pound with a heavy object, such as a 450 ml can of tomatoes, a hammer or a rolling pin. Alternatively, some food processors, blenders and hand-held blenders have a strong enough motor to crush ice; check the manufacturer's instructions.

To toast coconut flakes, place a frying pan over medium heat until smoking. Add coconut flakes and toss for 1 minute. Remove from heat. Alternatively, spread flakes onto a baking tray and place under a hot grill, or into a pre-heated 200°C oven, for 2–3 minutes.

A mortar and pestle is great for pounding small quantities of nuts and seeds, as well as spices. Many spices are best when freshly ground; the aromatic oils released give spicier, sweeter flavours. Buy only small amounts of spices and store them in a dark cupboard in airtight containers.

Nuts are best kept fresh in the freezer in an airtight container. To toast nuts, preheat a heavy frying pan over medium heat. Add the nuts and toss continually until lightly browned. Alternatively, spread nuts on a baking tray and place under a hot grill, or into a 200°C oven, and toast until lightly browned. Some nuts, such as pine nuts and peanuts, have a particularly high oil content and will therefore brown more quickly than others.

To extract the juices from a stalk of lemongrass, bruise it by crushing the white part with a rolling pin or in a mortar and pestle.

If available, use freshly grated coconut instead of desiccated coconut for a superior flavour. To crack open a coconut, first remove the milk by pushing a skewer through the coconut eyes and allowing the milk to drain into a container. (Use the coconut milk in smoothies or fruit juices.) Freeze the coconut for 30–60 minutes to loosen the flesh from the shell. Gently tap the coconut in several places with a hammer until it breaks. Scoop out the flesh and use.

The best way to freeze bananas is peeled and chopped into chunks. Place the pieces into freezer bags for easy use.

To make a delicious fruit slushy, freeze a smoothie or fruit juice, allow to defrost slightly, then blend in a food processor.

A splash of herbal tea can really liven up fresh fruit juices. Pour leftover or extra herbal tea into an ice-cube tray and freeze. When solid, transfer to a freezer container and label. Mint tea, green tea and lemongrass tea are a few good ones to have in the freezer.

To brew fresh herbal teas use a clean coffee plunger.

To remove blackberry, strawberry or raspberry seeds before making a smoothie, blend the fruit and then strain it through a fine sieve.

To remove the skins from apricots, peaches and tomatoes, blanch the fruit in boiling water for 1–2 minutes. Remove and refresh under cold water. Use a small fruit knife to gently peel off the skin.

When using fresh herbs, such as mint and parsley, juice the stalks as well as the leaves for extra flavour, vitamins and minerals. If you have picked the herbs from your own garden you may find the stalks are quite woody; if so, use only the soft green parts of the herb.

To peel a fresh mango, cut into the flesh with a sharp knife all the way to the stone and draw your knife in a complete circle around the fruit. Do the same the other way to make to make four equal quarters. Carefully slide the knife along the stone to remove the flesh and then scoop out the flesh from the skin using a spoon.

When you are spooning honey, spray or wipe a little light olive oil over the spoon first. This allows the honey to run off the spoon easily.

When washing fruits and vegetables, add a little apple cider vinegar to the water to help remove residual pesticides or herbicides.

# Fruit Juices

A beautiful display of fruit at the greengrocer's is a great reminder of the enormous variety of produce available. Year-round staples, such as oranges, apples, pears and lemons, are perennially delicious and combine well with some of the seasonal fruits, such as mango, grapes and guava, to make more exotic and special drinks.

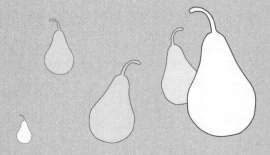

## Apple, orange and beetroot

Makes about 500 ml (serves 2)
2 large apples, quartered and cored
1 large orange, peeled (but with some white pith remaining) and halved
1 beetroot with tops removed, scrubbed and cut into chunks

Using an electric juicer, process the apple, orange and beetroot.
Serve immediately.


## Apple, pear and golden kiwifruit

Makes about 450 ml (serves 2)
1 large Granny Smith apple, quartered and cored
1 large ripe nashi pear, quartered and cored
2 golden kiwifruit, peeled and halved

Using an electric juicer, process the apple, pear and kiwifruit.
Serve immediately.

## Apple, pear and honeydew melon

**Makes about 500 ml (serves 2)**
2 Granny Smith apples, quartered and cored
2 ripe pears, quartered and cored
300 g honeydew melon, peeled, deseeded and cut into chunks

Using an electric juicer, process the apple, pear and melon.
Serve immediately.


## Grape and celery

**Makes about 300 ml (serves 1–2)**
1 cup seedless white grapes, removed from stems
3 sticks celery, cut into chunks

Using an electric juicer, process the grapes and celery.
Serve immediately.

## Grape, cucumber, apple and mint

**Makes about 500 ml (serves 2)**
2 cups seedless white grapes, removed from stems
1 large Lebanese cucumber, cut into chunks
2 green apples, quartered and cored
5 sprigs mint

Using an electric juicer, process the grapes, cucumber, apple and mint. Serve immediately.


## Grape and lime

**Makes about 100 ml (serves 1)**
2 cups seedless black grapes, removed from stems
1 small wedge lime, peeled

Using an electric juicer, process the grapes and lime. Serve immediately, poured over ice.

## Grapefruit, orange, beetroot and ginger

Makes about 450 ml (serves 2)
1 large pink grapefruit, peeled (but with some white pith remaining)
   and quartered
1 large orange, peeled (but with some white pith remaining) and halved
1 beetroot with tops removed, scrubbed and cut into chunks
1 small (2 cm) knob fresh ginger, peeled

Using an electric juicer, process the citrus fruits, beetroot and
ginger. Serve immediately.


## Grapefruit and strawberry

Makes about 300 ml (serves 1–2)
1 large pink grapefruit, peeled (but with some white pith remaining)
   and quartered
4 large strawberries, hulled

Using an electric juicer, process the grapefruit and strawberries.
Serve immediately.

## Guava and orange

**Makes about 200 ml (serves 1)**
2 ripe guavas, peeled and cut into chunks
2 large oranges, peeled (but with some white pith remaining) and halved

Using an electric juicer, process the guava and orange.
Serve immediately, poured over ice.

## Guava, orange and ruby red grapefruit

**Makes about 400 ml (serves 2)**
2 ripe guavas, peeled and cut into chunks
1 orange, peeled (but with some white pith remaining) and halved
1 red ruby grapefruit, peeled (but with some white pith remaining)
    and halved

Using an electric juicer, process the guava, orange and grapefruit.
Serve immediately.

## Honeydew melon and golden kiwifruit

Makes about 250 ml (serves 1)
300 g honeydew melon, peeled, deseeded and cut into chunks
3 golden kiwifruit, peeled and halved

Using an electric juicer, process the melon and kiwifruit.
Serve immediately.


## Honeydew melon and mint cooler

Makes about 200 ml (serves 1)
300 g honeydew melon, peeled, deseeded and cut into chunks
2 sprigs mint

Using an electric juicer, process the melon and mint.
Serve immediately.

## Honeydew melon, mint and ginger

Makes about 200 ml (serves 1)
300 g honeydew melon, peeled, deseeded and cut into chunks
2 sprigs mint
1 small (2 cm) knob fresh ginger, peeled

Using an electric juicer, process the melon, mint and ginger.
Serve immediately.


## Honeydew melon, orange and strawberry

Makes about 250 ml (serves 1)
200 g honeydew melon, peeled, deseeded and cut into chunks
1 orange, peeled (but with some white pith remaining) and halved
6 large strawberries, hulled

Using an electric juicer, process the melon, orange and strawberries.
Serve immediately.

## Orange, lemon, mandarin and strawberry

**Makes about 300 ml (serves 1–2)**
1 orange, peeled (but with some white pith remaining) and halved
1 small lemon, peeled (but with some white pith remaining) and halved
1 mandarin, peeled and halved
3 large strawberries, hulled

Using an electric juicer, process the citrus fruits and strawberries.
Serve immediately.

## Orange and mango

**Makes about 500 ml (serves 2)**
2 large oranges, peeled (but with some white pith remaining) and halved
½ large mango, peeled and cut into chunks

Using an electric juicer, process the orange and mango.
Serve immediately

## Orange, pineapple, carrot and ginger

Makes about 500 ml (serves 2)
3 oranges, peeled (but with some white pith remaining) and halved
300 g pineapple flesh, cut into chunks
3 carrots, chopped
1 small (2 cm) knob fresh ginger, peeled

Using an electric juicer, process the orange, pineapple, carrot and ginger. Serve immediately.


## Pawpaw, strawberry and lime

Makes about 200 ml (serves 1)
½ medium red pawpaw, peeled and cut into chunks
125 g strawberries, hulled
½ small lime, peeled (but with some white pith remaining)

Using an electric juicer, process the pawpaw, strawberries and lime. Serve immediately.

## Pear, fennel and mint

Makes about 350 ml (serves 1–2)
2 large ripe pears, quartered and cored
1 large bulb fennel, quartered
8 sprigs mint

Using an electric juicer, process the pear, fennel and mint.
Serve immediately.


## Pear, grape, lime and ginger

Makes about 250 ml (serves 1)
1 ripe nashi pear, quartered and cored
1 cup seedless white grapes, removed from stems
1 small wedge lime, peeled
1 small (2 cm) knob fresh ginger, peeled

Using an electric juicer, process the pear, grapes,
lime and ginger. Serve immediately.

## Pear and lemon

**Makes about 300 ml (serves 1–2)**
2 large ripe pears, quartered and cored
½ small lemon, peeled (but with some white pith remaining)

Using an electric juicer, process the pear and lemon.
Serve immediately.


## Pear, lemon, mint and ginger

**Makes about 450 ml (serves 2)**
2 large ripe nashi pears, quartered and cored
½ small lemon, peeled (but with some white pith remaining)
6 sprigs mint
1 small (2 cm) knob fresh ginger, peeled

Using an electric juicer, process the pear, lemon, mint and ginger.
Serve immediately.

## Pear, mint and ginger

Makes about 350 ml (serves 1–2)

3 large ripe pears, quartered and cored

7 sprigs mint

1 large (4 cm) knob fresh ginger, peeled

Using an electric juicer, process the pear, mint and ginger.
Serve immediately.


## Pineapple, apple and mint

Makes about 600 ml (serves 2–3)

300 g pineapple flesh, cut into chunks

3 Granny Smith apples, quartered and cored

4 sprigs mint

Using an electric juicer, process the pineapple, apple and mint.
Serve immediately, poured over ice.

## Pineapple, apple and mint with ginger

Makes about 400 ml (serves 2)
200 g pineapple flesh, cut into chunks
1 large apple, quartered and cored
4 sprigs mint
1 small (2 cm) knob fresh ginger, peeled

Using an electric juicer, process the pineapple, apple,
mint and ginger. Serve immediately.

## Pineapple, banana passionfruit and mint

Makes about 250 ml (serves 1)
200 g pineapple flesh, cut into chunks
4 banana passionfruit, pulp only
4 sprigs mint

Using an electric juicer, process the pineapple, passionfruit
pulp and mint. Serve immediately.

## Pineapple, honeydew melon and apple

Makes about 600 ml (serves 2–3)
300 g pineapple flesh, cut into chunks
300 g honeydew melon, peeled, deseeded and cut into chunks
3 Granny Smith apples, quartered and cored

Using an electric juicer, process the pineapple, melon and apple.
Serve immediately, poured over ice.

## Pomegranate and lime

Makes about 200 ml (serves 1)
2 ripe pomegranates, halved
2 limes, halved
sugar, to taste

Squeeze the pomegranate halves using a citrus juicer and set
the juice aside. Clean the juicer, then squeeze the limes. Mix the
fruit juices together, sweeten with a little sugar to taste and serve
immediately, poured over crushed ice.

## Rockmelon, mulberry, mint and parsley

Makes about 400 ml (serves 2)
400 g rockmelon (cantaloupe), peeled, deseeded and cut into chunks
1 cup sweet mulberries
2 sprigs mint
½ cup parsley

Using an electric juicer, process the melon, mulberries,
mint and parsley. Serve immediately.


## Rockmelon, orange and mint

Makes about 250 ml (serves 1)
200 g rockmelon (cantaloupe), peeled, deseeded and cut into chunks
1 large orange, peeled (but with some white pith remaining) and halved
4 sprigs mint

Using an electric juicer, process the melon, orange and mint.
Serve immediately.

## Watermelon, green grape and cucumber

**Makes about 450 ml (serves 2)**
400 g watermelon flesh, cut into chunks
1 cup green seedless grapes, removed from stems
200 g cucumber, cut into chunks

Using an electric juicer, process the watermelon, grapes
and cucumber. Serve immediately.


## Watermelon, strawberry and mint

**Makes about 450 ml (serves 2)**
400 g seedless watermelon flesh, cut into chunks
4 large strawberries, hulled
6 sprigs mint

Using an electric juicer, process the watermelon, strawberries
and mint. Serve immediately.

## Watermelon, tangelo, strawberry and ginger

**Makes about 400 ml (serves 2)**
300 g seedless watermelon flesh, cut into chunks
1 tangelo, peeled (but with some pith remaining) and halved
4 large strawberries, hulled
1 small (2 cm) knob fresh ginger, peeled

Using an electric juicer, process the watermelon, tangelo, strawberries and ginger. Serve immediately.

# Vegetable Juices

A vegetable juice is like a fresh salad in a glass; and, as with a salad, when composing a veggie juice, you can mix together lots of different herbs and vegetables that will produce anything from an earthy sweet flavour to something a bit peppery with a little spice. Vegetable staples, such as carrots and celery, and herbs, such as parsley, make a great base for a juice, to which more seasonal vegetables can be added. The fun is experimenting with a whole variety of vegetables, which will lead you to discover fresh, healthy and delicious combinations.

## Asparagus, lettuce, celery and cucumber

*Iceberg is an easy lettuce to portion due to its tightly folded leaves; remove the outer leaves, then simply cut off a chunk. This juice is particularly refreshing served over ice in a tall glass.*

**Makes about 400 ml (serves 2)**
6 spears raw asparagus, cut into chunks
50 g iceberg lettuce, cut into chunks
3 sticks celery, cut into chunks
1 Lebanese cucumber, cut into chunks

Using an electric juicer, process the asparagus, lettuce, celery and cucumber. Serve immediately.

## Beetroot, carrot and apple

Makes about 300 ml (serves 1–2)
2 large beetroots including tops, scrubbed and cut into chunks
2 carrots, cut into chunks
1 large apple, quartered and cored

Using an electric juicer, process the beetroot, carrot and apple.
Serve immediately.

## Beetroot, celery, apple and garlic
*In this juice, the sweet earthiness of the beetroot and apple
goes well with the heat of the garlic.*

Makes about 500 ml (serves 2)
2 large beetroots including tops, scrubbed and cut into chunks
2 sticks celery, cut into chunks
2 apples, quartered and cored
2 cloves garlic, peeled

Using an electric juicer, process the beetroot, celery, apple
and garlic. Serve immediately.

## Beetroot and orange

*The acid of the citrus cuts through the sweetness of the beetroot,*
*making this favourite juice refreshing and cleansing.*

**Makes about 400 ml (serves 2)**

1 large beetroot including top, scrubbed and cut into chunks
2 oranges, peeled (but with some white pith remaining) and halved

Using an electric juicer, process the beetroot and orange.
Serve immediately.

## Beetroot, tomato and orange

**Makes about 500 ml (serves 2)**

2 beetroots including some tops, scrubbed and cut into chunks
2 tomatoes, cut into chunks
1 large orange, peeled (but with some white pith remaining) and halved

Using an electric juicer, process the beetroot, tomato and orange.
Serve immediately.

## Cabbage and carrot

Makes about 300 ml (serves 1–2)

400 g cabbage, cut into chunks

4 carrots, cut into chunks

Using an electric juicer, process the cabbage and carrot. Serve immediately.


## Cabbage, carrot, celery and apple

*Like a glass of coleslaw – without the dressing.*

Makes about 300 ml (serves 1–2)

200 g cabbage, cut into chunks

2 carrots, cut into chunks

2 sticks celery, cut into chunks

1 apple, quartered and cored

Using an electric juicer, process the cabbage, carrot, celery and apple. Serve immediately.

## Capsicum, lettuce, parsley and chilli

*In this juice, the sweet, fruity capsicum with a hint of chilli
is enough to lift the palate and refresh the mouth.*

**Makes about 500 ml (serves 2)**
1 large red capsicum, deseeded and cut into chunks
1 large yellow capsicum, deseeded and cut into chunks
100 g iceberg lettuce, cut into chunks
6 sprigs curly parsley
½ small red chilli, deseeded and finely chopped

Using an electric juicer, process the capsicums, lettuce and parsley.
Stir in chilli to taste, and serve immediately over ice.

## Carrot, alfalfa, lettuce and ginger

*For a cool drink, chill the ingredients before juicing them.*

**Makes about 250 ml (serves 1)**
3 carrots, cut into chunks
125 g alfalfa sprouts
100 g iceberg lettuce, cut into chunks
1 small (2 cm) knob fresh ginger, peeled

Using an electric juicer, process the carrot, alfalfa, lettuce and ginger. Serve immediately.

## Carrot, celery, lettuce and parsley

**Makes about 250 ml (serves 1)**
2 carrots, cut into chunks
3 sticks celery including tops, cut into chunks
100 g iceberg lettuce, cut into chunks
7 sprigs curly parsley

Using an electric juicer, process the carrot, celery, lettuce and parsley. Serve immediately.

## Carrot and orange

*This all-time favourite juice is a great way start to the day.*

Makes about 300 ml (serves 1–2)

4 carrots, cut into chunks

2 small oranges, peeled (but with some white pith remaining)
and halved

Using an electric juicer, process the carrot and orange.
Serve immediately.


## Carrot, spinach and apple

Makes about 300 ml (serves 1–2)

4 carrots, cut into chunks

100 g spinach, trimmed, washed and chopped

1 apple, quartered and cored

Using an electric juicer, process the carrot, spinach and apple.
Serve immediately.

## Celery and apple

Makes about 400 ml (serves 2)
½ head celery with tops removed, cut into chunks
2 large green apples, quartered and cored

Using an electric juicer, process the celery and apple.
Serve immediately.


## Celery, carrot and apple

Makes about 400 ml (serves 2)
3 sticks celery including tops, cut into chunks
1 large carrot, cut into chunks
1 green apple, quartered and cored

Using an electric juicer, process the celery, carrot and apple.
Serve immediately.

## Cucumber, capsicum, celery, parsley and mint

**Makes about 300 ml (serves 1–2)**
2 Lebanese cucumbers, cut into chunks
1 green capsicum, deseeded and cut into chunks
2 sticks celery including tops, cut into chunks
2 sprigs curly parsley
4 sprigs mint

Using an electric juicer, process the cucumber, capsicum, celery, parsley and mint. Serve immediately.

## Cucumber, carrot and apple

**Makes about 300 ml (serves 1–2)**
2 Lebanese cucumbers, cut into chunks
2 large carrots, cut into chunks
1 green apple, quartered and cored

Using an electric juicer, process the cucumber, carrot and apple. Serve immediately.

## Fennel, apple and ginger

Makes about 500 ml (serves 2)

2 bulbs fennel, quartered

2 Granny Smith apples, quartered and cored

1 small (2 cm) knob fresh ginger, peeled

Using an electric juicer, process the fennel, apple and ginger.
Serve immediately.

## Lettuce, apple and mint

Makes about 250 ml (serves 1)

½ cos lettuce, roughly chopped

1 large Granny Smith apple, quartered and cored

6 sprigs mint

Using an electric juicer, process the lettuce, apple and mint.
Serve immediately.

## Lettuce, apple and parsley

*A tasty green juice with the parsley adding a hint of earthiness.*

Makes about 350 ml (serves 1–2)

½ cos lettuce, roughly chopped

2 Granny Smith apples, quartered and cored

1 small bunch curly parsley

Using an electric juicer, process the lettuce, apple and parsley. Serve immediately.


## Spinach, apple and ginger

*A bright green juice full of antioxidants and calcium.*

Makes about 300 ml (serves 1–2)

400 g silverbeet, trimmed, washed and chopped

2 apples, quartered and cored

1 small (2 cm) knob fresh ginger, peeled

Using an electric juicer, process the spinach, apple and ginger. Serve immediately.

## Tomato, capsicum, carrot, lime and mint

Makes about 400 ml (serves 2)

2 large tomatoes, cut into chunks

1 large red capsicum, deseeded and cut into chunks

1 carrot, cut into chunks

1 small wedge lime, peeled

3 sprigs mint

Using an electric juicer, process the tomato, capsicum, carrot, lime and mint. Serve immediately.

## Tomato, capsicum, celery, cucumber and chilli

*This juice has the refreshing taste of a summer salad. By adding
a little chilli, the flavour is transformed to that of a spicy Mexican
salsa.*

**Makes about 400 ml (serves 2)**

2 large tomatoes, cut into chunks

1 red capsicum, deseeded and cut into chunks

3 sticks celery, cut into chunks

1 Lebanese cucumber, cut into chunks

½ small red chilli, deseeded and finely chopped (optional)

Using an electric juicer, process the tomato, capsicum, celery
and cucumber. Stir in the chilli, if desired, and serve immediately.

## Tomato and orange

**Makes about 300 ml (serves 1–2)**
2 large tomatoes, cut into chunks
2 large oranges, peeled (but with some white pith remaining)
    and quartered

Using an electric juicer, process the tomato and orange.
Serve immediately.


## Watercress, celery and grape

*The grapes add a delicious sweetness to this juice and balance
out the spiciness of the watercress.*

**Makes about 300 ml (serves 1–2)**
2 cups watercress leaves, including some stalks
4 sticks celery, cut into chunks
1 cup seedless white grapes, removed from stems

Using an electric juicer, process the watercress, celery and grapes.
Serve immediately.

## Watercress, orange and fennel

*Spicy watercress and sweet fennel and orange makes a refreshing combination.*

Makes about 250 ml (serves 1)
2 cups watercress leaves, including some stalks
2 oranges, peeled (but with some white pith remaining) and halved
1 bulb fennel, quartered

Using an electric juicer, process the watercress, orange and fennel. Serve immediately.

# Smoothies

When it comes to a delicious, healthy and filling snack, you can't beat the versatile smoothie for taste and calcium. The calcium component can be supplied by anything from regular milk to calcium-fortified soy milk, rice milk or oat milk, to soy acidophilus yoghurt. You can even use silken tofu for a taste that's just a bit different (but bear in mind that tofu has a lower calcium content than most other dairy or calcium-fortified non-dairy products). Coconut milk or coconut cream can add an exotic taste when blended with particular tropical fruits; and buttermilk is a low-fat, high-calcium dairy product that is delicious in smoothies and combines well with low-fat plain yoghurt.

If you prefer your smoothie at the end of a meal, as a dessert, then think about adding ice-cream, fruit sorbet, silken tofu or low-fat ricotta in place of the dairy component.

Smoothies can also be thickened by adding banana, nuts or oatmeal. Put a few bananas in the freezer for later, or keep frozen berries on hand to make a thick fruit slush – delicious with yoghurt or tofu.

Natural sweeteners, such as honey, can add to the taste of a simple smoothie. Other sweeteners include maple syrup, apple juice concentrate, powdered fructose and dark and pale palm sugar – each will add a rich, unusual sweet taste to your drink. Be aware that some smoothies will be sweet enough from the natural fruits; extra sweeteners should only be added after tasting.

There are many ingredients that can add texture, taste and additional health benefits to a smoothie or juice, and the following list is a starting point only. Try the recipes in this chapter and then experiment with your favourite flavours and the ingredients to follow. (Note: measurements are a guide only.)

**Almond milk** – a good non-dairy base for smoothies; see recipe on page 73

**Bee pollen** – contains proteins and vitamins A, B, C and E; use ¼ tablespoon per 250 ml of liquid; it is advised that asthmatics and those allergic to bee stings never use this product

**Blackstrap molasses** – made from sugar cane and a great source of calcium and iron; use 1 teaspoon per 250 ml of liquid

**Brewers yeast** – contains protein and vitamin B; use 1 teaspoon per 250 ml of liquid

**Cardamom** – aids digestion; use ½ teaspoon ground cardamom per 250 ml of liquid; whole cardamom pods can be used for making teas

**Carob** – contains no caffeine and is therefore a good substitute for cocoa and chocolate as an energy carbohydrate; use 1 tablespoon carob powder per 250 ml of liquid

**Cinnamon** – aids digestion; sprinkle a pinch of ground cinnamon on top of smoothies

**Coconut** – adds a tropical taste; stir in desiccated coconut before serving; use 1 tablespoon per 500 ml of liquid

**Glucosamine powder** – a health additive that aids the repair of cartilage; use 1 tablespoon per 250 ml of liquid

**Ground almonds** – adds flavour, acts as a thickener and is a rich source of calcium; use 1 tablespoon per 250 ml of liquid

**Honey** – has antioxidant properties; use 1 tablespoon per 250 ml of liquid, or to taste

**Lecithin** – an extract from soya beans; used as an emulsifier, it is also useful to liver function, memory and the nervous system (make sure the product is made from GE-free soya beans)

**Linseed (flaxseed) meal** – a good source of omega-3 fatty acids; grind the seeds as needed, using a spice grinder or food processor; use 1 teaspoon per 250 ml of liquid

**LSA mix** – a blend of natural protein and fibre, which usually includes linseeds (flaxseeds), sunflower kernels, almond kernels

**Nutmeg** – aids the relief of flatulence; add a pinch, or to taste, to non-dairy based smoothies

**Palm sugar** – an alternative sweetener to sugar, made from coconut sap; the darker the sugar, the more caramel the flavour; it is often sold in solid cakes that can be shaved or crumbled; use 1 tablespoon per 250 ml of liquid

**Peanut butter** – adds a nutty flavour; use peanut butter containing no additives, such as salt; use ½ tablespoon per 250 ml of liquid

**Protein whey powder** – a good source of amino acids; use 1 tablespoon per 250 ml of liquid

**Pure maple syrup** – an alternative sweetener to honey; contains calcium and thiamine; use 1 tablespoon per 250 ml of liquid

**Psyllium husks** – aids waste removal; use 1 teaspoon per 250 ml of liquid

**Sesame seeds** – contain calcium, potassium and magnesium; use 1 teaspoon per 250 ml of liquid

**Slippery elm powder** – soothing to the digestive system; use 2 teaspoons per 250 ml of liquid

**Spirulina** – rich in chlorophyll and betacarotene; available in powder or flakes; use ¼ teaspoon per 250 ml of liquid

**Sunflower seed meal** – contains vitamin E and zinc; use 1 tablespoon per 250 ml of liquid

**Tahini** – a paste made from sesame seeds; contains calcium (note: unhulled tahini paste has more calcium than the paler hulled paste); use 1 tablespoon per 250 ml of liquid

**Vanilla extract** – adds flavour; use ¼ teaspoon per 250 ml of liquid

**Wheat germ** – contains vitamin E and thiamine; use 1 tablespoon per 250 ml of liquid

**Yoghurt** – good source of B vitamins, protein and calcium, and helps keep the friendly bacteria in the intestine well balanced; check label for extra starter cultures, such as Lactobacillus acidophilus and Bifidobacteria bacterium, which can enhance health benefits

## Almond Milk

*This creamy drink is high in protein and is terrific both by itself and as the base of a smoothie.*

**Makes about 250 ml (serves 1)**
100 g ground almonds
1 cup ice cubes
honey, to taste
250 ml iced water

Place the ground almonds and ice cubes in a blender or food processor and blend. Add honey to taste. With the motor running, slowly pour in the iced water and process until smooth. Strain and discard the ground nuts, and pour the milk into a tall glass over ice.

## Apricot and almond smoothie

Makes about 300 ml (serves 1–2)
6 apricots, de-stoned and cut into chunks
2 tablespoons ground almonds
250 ml low-fat milk
100 ml low-fat plain yoghurt
1 teaspoon honey, or to taste
1 teaspoon toasted almond flakes

Place all the ingredients except the almond flakes into a blender or food processor and blend until smooth. Pour into a glass, then sprinkle with the almond flakes.

## Avocado smoothie

*This thick smoothie is a meal in itself and the nutty taste of soy milk makes a great base. Use soy yoghurt instead of plain yoghurt, if preferred.*

**Makes about 500 ml (serves 2)**
1 large avocado, peeled and cut into chunks
3 tablespoons freshly squeezed lemon juice
2 tablespoons lemon zest
300 ml soy milk
2 tablespoons plain yoghurt
1–2 tablespoons honey, or to taste

Place all the ingredients into a blender or food processor and blend until smooth. If the smoothie is too thick, stir through a little water. Pour into glasses over ice and serve with a spoon.

## Avocado and pineapple smoothie

*The refreshing tastes of lime and pineapple make this*
*avocado smoothie a perfect ice-cool treat.*

**Makes about 600 ml (serves 2–3)**
1 small avocado, peeled and cut into chunks
150 g pineapple flesh, cut into chunks
2 tablespoons freshly squeezed lime juice
2 tablespoons low-fat plain yoghurt
125 ml soy milk
1 cup crushed ice
mineral water (optional)

Place all the ingredients except the mineral water into a blender or
food processor and blend until smooth. If the smoothie is too thick,
stir through a little mineral water. Pour into glasses and serve.

## Banana, carob and peanut smoothie

*A rich and filling smoothie for any time of the day. Notice how the slightly acidic buttermilk cuts through the sweetness of the banana and honey.*

Makes about 300 ml (serves 1–2)
1 large banana, peeled and cut into chunks
1 tablespoon carob powder
1 tablespoon peanut butter
250 ml buttermilk
2 teaspoons honey, or to taste

Place all the ingredients into a blender or food processor and blend until smooth. Pour into glasses and serve with a spoon.

## Banana and passionfruit smoothie

Makes about 400 ml (serves 2)
1 frozen banana, peeled and cut into chunks
250 ml soy milk
1 tablespoon ground almonds
1 tablespoon honey
2 passionfruit, pulp only

Place all the ingredients except the passionfruit pulp into a blender
or food processor and blend until smooth. Stir in the passionfruit
pulp and pour into glasses.

# Banana and strawberry smoothie

**Makes about 300 ml (serves 1–2)**
1 frozen banana, peeled and cut into chunks
6 strawberries, hulled and halved
125 ml buttermilk
125 ml vanilla yoghurt

Place all the ingredients into a blender or food processor and
blend until smooth and creamy. Pour into tall glasses and serve
with a spoon.

## Banana, tahini and fig smoothie

*This high-calcium, rich and filling smoothie is perfect for lunch or for when you need an afternoon energy boost.*

Makes about 600 ml (serves 2–3)

1 banana, peeled and cut into chunks
2 tablespoons tahini
200 ml soy milk
80 ml low-fat yoghurt
4 finely chopped fresh figs or ¼ cup finely chopped dried figs

Place all the ingredients except the figs into a blender or food processor and blend until smooth. Stir in the figs, then pour into glasses.

## Carob soy smoothie

*This smoothie suits a midmorning non-caffeine break. However, if you do need that hit, substitute cocoa for the carob powder and add more honey to taste.*

**Makes about 300 ml (serves 1–2)**
1 tablespoon carob powder
100 g silken tofu
200 ml soy milk
½–1 tablespoon dark honey, or to taste
large pinch freshly grated nutmeg

Place all the ingredients into a blender or food processor and blend until smooth. Pour into tall glasses and serve with a spoon.

# Cranberry and blackberry smoothie

Makes about 500 ml (serves 2)
200 g cranberries, fresh or defrosted
200 ml cranberry juice
100 g silken tofu
2 teaspoons honey or maple syrup
100 g blackberries, fresh or defrosted

Place all the ingredients except for the blackberries into a blender
or food processor and blend until smooth. Stir in the blackberries,
then pour into glasses.

## Grape and orange smoothie

*Seedless black currant grapes are the key to this smoothie.*
*Keep a special eye out for them when they are in season –*
*you won't be disappointed.*

**Makes about 300 ml (serves 1–2)**
2 cups seedless black grapes, removed from stems
2 oranges, peeled (but with some white pith remaining) and halved
200 ml vanilla yoghurt

Using an electric juicer, process the grapes and orange. Stir
in the yoghurt, then pour into glasses.

## Mango and cardamom lassi

*A classic Indian smoothie with the exotic taste of ground cardamom.*

**Makes about 500 ml (serves 2)**

1 small mango, peeled and cut into chunks
125 ml low-fat plain yoghurt
125 ml milk
½ teaspoon freshly ground cardamom seeds
1 tablespoon palm sugar
1 cup crushed ice

Place all the ingredients into a blender or food processor and blend until smooth. Pour into long glasses over extra crushed ice.

## Mango and passionfruit smoothie

*Lime and mango is a refreshing combination, and the addition of yoghurt, coconut and passionfruit gives this smoothie a truly South Seas flavour.*

**Makes about 250 ml (serves 1)**
1 small mango, peeled and cut into chunks
2 tablespoons freshly squeezed lime juice
125 ml plain yoghurt
1 tablespoon desiccated coconut
1 passionfruit, pulp only

Place all the ingredients except the passionfruit pulp into a blender or food processor and blend until smooth and creamy. Stir in the passionfruit pulp, then pour into a glass.

## Mango and peach smoothie

Makes about 450 ml (serves 2)
1 large mango, peeled and cut into chunks
2 peaches, de-stoned and cut into chunks
125 ml plain yoghurt
250 ml low-fat milk
1 tablespoon desiccated coconut

Place all the ingredients into a blender or food processor
and blend until smooth. Pour into tall glasses.

## Orange, apricot and pawpaw smoothie

*Dried apricots are not too sweet and they add an interesting texture and flavour to this smoothie.*

**Makes about 500 ml (serves 2)**

2 oranges, freshly squeezed
¼ cup dried apricots
200 g pawpaw, peeled, deseeded and cut into chunks
3 tablespoons low-fat plain yoghurt

Place all the ingredients into a blender or food processor and blend until smooth. Pour into tall glasses.

## Orange and carob smoothie

Makes about 300 ml (serves 1–2)
2 oranges, freshly squeezed
1 teaspoon grated orange rind
1 tablespoon carob powder
200 ml low-fat plain yoghurt
1 tablespoon maple syrup, or to taste

Place the orange juice, orange rind, carob powder and yoghurt into a blender or food processor and blend until smooth. Sweeten with maple syrup to taste.

## Peach and almond smoothie

*The tang of buttermilk and the sweetness of peaches make this smoothie a refreshing boost.*

**Makes about 500 ml (serves 2)**

6 fresh peaches, de-stoned and cut into chunks

2 tablespoons ground almonds

200 ml plain yoghurt

250 ml buttermilk

Place all the ingredients into a blender or food processor and blend until smooth. Pour into glasses and serve with a spoon.

## Peach and passionfruit smoothie

Makes about 400 ml (serves 2)
2 white peaches, de-stoned and cut into chunks
125 ml soy milk
100 g silken tofu
3 large passionfruit, pulp only
1 teaspoon honey, or to taste

Place the peach, soy milk and tofu into a blender or food processor and blend until smooth. Stir in the passionfruit pulp and honey, then pour into glasses.

## Pina Colada cooler

*A favourite tropical drink on a balmy summer's day. Serve with a wedge of lime on the side of the glass.*

**Makes about 500 ml (serves 2)**
1 small mango, peeled and cut into chunks
100 g pineapple flesh, cut into chunks
1 lime, freshly squeezed
200 ml coconut milk
1 cup crushed ice

Place all the ingredients into a blender or food processor and blend until smooth. Pour into tall glasses over extra crushed ice.

## Pineapple, pawpaw and strawberry smoothie

*Dark palm sugar adds a hint of caramel to this smoothie, and goes well with pineapple and pawpaw.*

**Makes about 500 ml (serves 2)**
250 g pineapple flesh, cut into chunks
½ pink pawpaw, peeled, deseeded and cut into chunks
150 g strawberries, hulled and halved
2 tablespoons dark palm sugar
200 ml rice milk

Place all the ingredients into a blender or food processor and blend until smooth. Pour into tall glasses over ice.

## Plum and blackberry smoothie

**Makes about 700 ml (serves 2–3)**
4 black plums, halved and de-stoned
50 g blackberries, fresh or defrosted
100 ml vanilla yoghurt
100 ml milk

Place all the ingredients in a blender or food processor
and blend until smooth. Pour into tall glasses.

## Rockmelon smoothie

*A delicious and filling shake that is rich in betacarotene.*

**Makes about 500 ml (serves 2)**
300 g rockmelon (cantaloupe), peeled, deseeded and cut into chunks
125 ml soy milk
200 g silken tofu
1 tablespoon dark honey
1 teaspoon vanilla extract

Place all the ingredients into a blender or food processor
and blend until smooth. Pour into tall glasses and serve.


## Rockmelon and orange smoothie

**Makes about 300 ml (serves 1–2)**
600 g rockmelon (cantaloupe), peeled, deseeded and cut into chunks
1 small orange, peeled (but with some white pith remaining) and halved
1 tablespoon plain yoghurt

Using an electric juicer, process the melon and orange. Whisk in the
yoghurt and pour into tall glasses.

## Summer fruit smoothie

*When cherries are in season, indulge a little by choosing the black variety, which are sweet and fleshy, and by buying fresh raspberries.*

**Makes about 500 ml (serves 2)**
1 banana, peeled and cut into chunks
1 cup dark cherries, pitted
½ cup fresh raspberries
250 ml low-fat milk
100 ml plain yoghurt

Place all the ingredients into a blender or food processor and blend until smooth. Pour into tall glasses.

## Tropical smoothie

*Start the day with a taste of the tropics.*

**Makes about 400 ml (serves 2)**
1 orange, freshly squeezed
200 g pineapple flesh, cut into chunks
½ small (2 cm) knob fresh ginger, peeled and grated
1 small frozen banana, peeled and cut into chunks
3 tablespoons coconut milk

Place all the ingredients into a blender or food processor
and blend until smooth. Pour into glasses over crushed ice.

# Rescues and Remedies

The reality of modern life is that we are often juggling work, a social life, sport and even a family – and all at an increasing pace. Because of this it can sometimes be hard to focus on the needs of our bodies, and, as a result, we may find ourselves in need of a health or energy boost. The following juices can help get busy people back on track.

## NATURAL CLEANSERS

The following three juices are great for helping you pick yourself up after a night of indulging! Each contains a whopping boost of electrolytes as well as a bit of sugar, which is essential when you are trying to re-hydrate. As well as drinking one of these juices, you should drink lots of water throughout the day.

## Carrot, apple, grapefruit and beetroot juice

*For the particularly delicate, this juice is easy to drink and soothing to the stomach. It is also nurturing to look at.*

**Makes about 300 ml (serves 1)**

1 large carrot, cut into chunks

1 apple, quartered and cored

1 small red ruby grapefruit or large blood orange, peeled (but with some white pith remaining) and quartered

1 small beetroot including some tops, scrubbed and cut into chunks

Using an electric juicer, process all the ingredients. Pour into a long glass and sip slowly through a straw.

## Carrot, apple, beetroot and red capsicum juice

*Refreshing in flavour, this juice also particularly aids liver function, helping your body to flush out toxins.*

**Makes about 300 ml (serves 1)**
2 carrots, cut into chunks
2 small apples, quartered and cored
1 small beetroot including some tops, scrubbed and cut into chunks
1 red capsicum, deseeded and cut into chunks
1 teaspoon lecithin (see page 70)

Using an electric juicer, process all the ingredients except the lecithin. Stir through the lecithin, then pour into a long glass and sip slowly through a straw.

## Kiwifruit, banana, soy and almond smoothie

*Settle your stomach with this concoction. The kiwifruit provides a good dose of vitamin C, which, it is claimed, helps clear alcohol out of your system.*

Makes about 300 ml (serves 1)
2 kiwifruit, peeled and cut into chunks
1 banana, peeled and cut into chunks
100 ml soy milk or rice milk
2 tablespoons ground almonds
1 tablespoons slippery elm powder (see page 72)

Place all the ingredients into a blender or food processor and blend until smooth. Pour into a glass.

## ENERGISERS

These drinks are good preparation for a long day ahead. A healthy, energising smoothie is an alternative to a cup of coffee or a chocolate bar. Any of the following smoothies can be made in the morning and taken to work or sport in a thermos or drink container. Keep cool and drink at morning or afternoon tea.

## Frozen berry, rice milk and honey smoothie

**Makes about 400 ml (serves 2)**
250 g frozen berries (strawberries, cranberries and/or blackberries)
250 ml rice milk
1 tablespoon honey
1 teaspoon wheat germ
1 teaspoon protein whey powder (see page 71)
2 tablespoons berry yoghurt, to serve

Place all the ingredients except the yoghurt into a blender or food processor and blend until smooth. Pour into tall glasses and top with a dollop of yoghurt.

## Pineapple, orange, coconut and yoghurt smoothie

Makes about 300 ml (serves 1–2)

2 oranges, freshly squeezed

200 g pineapple flesh, cut into chunks

½ cup freshly grated coconut or ⅓ cup desiccated coconut

3 tablespoons ground almonds

200 ml low-fat plain yoghurt

lime wedges, to serve

Place the orange juice, pineapple, coconut, ground almonds and yoghurt into a blender or food processor and blend until smooth. Pour into tall glasses and serve topped with a squeeze of lime.

## Banana, strawberry and orange smoothie with wheat germ

*This combination of ingredients offers the perfect snack. The LSA mix and wheat germ, which is rich in vitamins E and B, balance well with vitamin C from the strawberries and orange juice.*

**Makes about 400 ml (serves 2)**
1 banana, peeled and cut into chunks
6 strawberries, hulled and halved
1 orange, freshly squeezed
100 ml soy yoghurt
1 tablespoon wheat germ
2 tablespoons LSA mix (see page 70)

Place all the ingredients into a blender or food processor and blend until smooth. Pour into tall glasses and serve.

## APPETISERS

The following refreshing natural appetisers contain mint, parsley or ginger, all of which encourage good digestion. Sometimes a jaded palate or appetite need a little excitement, and these refreshers can provide just that. They make a lovely, stimulating drink before a rich meal.

## Pawpaw, ginger and mint refresher

Makes about 400 ml (serves 2)
375 g red or yellow pawpaw, peeled, deseeded and cut into chunks
1 small (2 cm) knob fresh ginger, peeled
3–4 sprigs mint
250 ml sparkling or still mineral water

Place the pawpaw, ginger and mint into a blender or food processor and blend until smooth. Stir in the mineral water and pour into glasses over ice.

## Pineapple, apple, ginger and mint refresher

Makes about 500 ml (serves 2)

300 g pineapple flesh, cut into chunks

1 apple, quartered and cored

1 small (2 cm) knob fresh ginger, peeled

2 sprigs mint

200 ml sparkling or still mineral water

Using an electric juicer, process the pineapple, apple, ginger and mint. Stir in the mineral water and pour into glasses over ice.

## Lettuce, celery, parsley and apple refresher

*Varieties of lettuce range from the common sweet round- or cabbage-shaped variety, such as butter lettuce and iceberg, to the long-leaf crisp variety, such as cos, and the frilly oak leaf. Any of these green lettuces would work well in this drink. Red-leaf lettuces are usually a little bitter and should be juiced with other sweeter ingredients.*

Makes about 250 ml (serves 1)

100 g iceberg or cos lettuce leaves, roughly chopped

2 sticks celery, cut into chunks

4 sprigs curly parsley

1 large green apple, quartered and cored

200 ml sparkling or still mineral water

Using an electric juicer, process the lettuce, celery, parsley and apple. Stir in the mineral water and pour into a glass over ice.

## VITAMIN C BOOSTS

These three recipes include a range of delicious fresh fruit and vegetables with high levels of vitamin C. Vitamin C aids many important body functions, including boosting the immune system, and has antiviral and antibacterial properties.

### Kiwifruit, orange and lemon refresher

Makes about 400 ml (serves 2)
4 kiwifruit, peeled and halved
1 orange, peeled (but with some white pith remaining) and halved
½ lemon, peeled (but with some white pith remaining) and halved
125 ml sparkling or still mineral water

Using an electric juicer, process the kiwifruit, orange and lemon. Stir in the sparkling mineral water and pour into tall glasses.

## Orange, mango, and rockmelon refresher

Makes about 400 ml (serves 2)
1 orange, peeled (but with some white pith remaining) and halved
1 small firm mango, peeled and cut into chunks
300 g rockmelon (cantaloupe), peeled, deseeded and cut into chunks
200 ml sparkling or still mineral water

Using an electric juicer, process the orange, mango and rockmelon. Stir in the mineral water and pour into tall glasses.

## Red capsicum, orange and tomato refresher

Makes about 500 ml (serves 2)
1 large red capsicum, deseeded and cut into chunks
1 orange, peeled (but with some white pith remaining) and halved
2 tomatoes, cut into chunks
125 ml sparkling or still mineral water

Using an electric juicer, process the capsicum, orange and tomato. Stir in the mineral water and pour into tall glasses over ice.

# Something Special

Taking the idea of preparing fresh juices to another culinary height, why not think of serving the following drinks for something a bit different – and healthy – at a special dinner party or on a picnic? Imaginative juices can be served instead of a cocktail, with or without a dash of alcohol. And shot glasses make the perfect vessel in which to serve a quick and tasty treat at a casual drinks party. Summer is a particularly good time to serve a cooling juice, and many of the recipes that follow can be prepared in advance and chilled, which is handy when entertaining a crowd. Make up a jug or fill up the thermos, get out the shot glasses, and prepare to be refreshed.

## SHOTS

A shot glass holds approximately 40–50 ml and is a great way to serve a small hit of a special drink. If the juice is quite thick, serve each shot on a small saucer with a teaspoon on the side.

## White Gazpacho

*The following two shots are based on the classic Spanish soup. Serve well chilled, in shot glasses to begin a brunch or dinner.*

**Makes about 350 ml (serves 6–7 shots)**
300 ml almond milk or rice milk
1 clove garlic, peeled and crushed
½–1 tablespoon apple cider vinegar, or to taste
3 tablespoons ground almonds
¼ teaspoon ground cumin
2 tablespoons toasted almond flakes, chopped
¼ cup seedless black grapes, removed from stems and chopped

Place the almond milk, garlic, vinegar and ground almonds into a blender or food processor and blend until smooth. Pour into an airtight container and chill, in the refrigerator, until ready to serve.

Pour into shot glasses, sprinkle each with toasted almonds and black grapes and serve immediately.

# Pink gazpacho

Makes about 600 ml (serves 12 shots)
6 ripe tomatoes, cut into chunks
2 cloves garlic, peeled and crushed
1 small red capsicum, deseeded and cut into chunks
1 small Spanish onion, peeled and cut into chunks
1–2 tablespoons apple cider vinegar
3 tablespoons ground almonds
pinch of sweet paprika
pinch of ground cumin
2 sticks celery, finely diced
1 Lebanese cucumber, peeled, deseeded and finely diced

Using an electric juicer, process the tomato, garlic, capsicum and
onion. Stir in the vinegar and ground almonds. In a bowl, mix the
spices with the celery and cucumber. Stir the mixture into the soup.
Pour into shot glasses and serve immediately. To store, pour into an
airtight container and chill, in the refrigerator, until ready to serve.

# Beetroot and yoghurt shots

Makes about 600 ml (serves 12 shots)
4 beetroots, scrubbed and cut into chunks
4 carrots, cut into chunks
½ Spanish onion, peeled and cut into chunks
¼ small lemon, peeled and with pith removed
200 ml plain yoghurt
100 ml still mineral water
1 tablespoon finely chopped dill
yoghurt, extra, to serve

Using an electric juicer, process the beetroot, carrot, onion and lemon. Whisk in the yoghurt, mineral water and dill. Pour into an airtight container and chill, in the refrigerator, until ready to serve.

Pour into shot glasses and garnish with a small dollop of yoghurt. Serve immediately.

## Spicy cucumber shots with chilli and mint

*These refreshing, spicy cucumber shots are best served freshly made. Chill all the ingredients before processing.*

**Makes about 600 ml (serves 12 shots)**

1 large cucumber, peeled, deseeded and cut into chunks

200 ml shop-bought tomato juice

250 ml still mineral water

200 ml low-fat plain yoghurt

½ teaspoon ground cumin

½ teaspoon ground coriander

1 clove garlic, peeled and crushed

1 green (salad) onion, cut into chunks

1 sprig mint, finely chopped

1 small red chilli, deseeded and finely chopped

freshly snipped chives, to serve

Place all the ingredients except the chives into a blender or food processor and blend until smooth. Pour into shot glasses, garnish with chives and serve immediately.

## Avocado shots with red capsicum salsa

*To give these shots extra heat, leave out the Tabasco sauce and add a little chopped fresh red chilli when you add the yoghurt.*

Makes about 600 ml (serves 12 shots)

1 large ripe avocado, peeled and cut into chunks

2 tablespoons freshly squeezed lime juice

1 clove garlic, peeled and crushed

1 teaspoon ground cumin

2 green (salad) onions, cut into chunks

250 ml still mineral water

250 ml low-fat plain yoghurt

¼ cup diced red capsicum

good dash of Tabasco sauce

2 tablespoons finely chopped coriander leaves

Place the avocado, lime juice, garlic, cumin, onion and mineral water into a blender or food processor and blend until smooth. Add the yoghurt and process again until combined. If the mixture is too thick, whiz through a little extra mineral water. Pour into an airtight container and chill, in the refrigerator, until ready to serve.

In a bowl, mix together the red capsicum, Tabasco sauce and coriander. Pour the avocado mixture into shot glasses and garnish with the chopped tomato salsa.

## Pawpaw sunset shots

*A summery tropical shot that goes well with a splash of tequila!*
*Pawpaw seeds are known to aid digestion so this is a good shot*
*to serve before a large dinner.*

Makes about 800 ml (serves 16 shots)

300 g red pawpaw, seeds removed and reserved, and flesh cut into
chunks

300 g pineapple flesh, cut into chunks

2 limes, freshly squeezed

100 ml still or sparking mineral water

1–2 tablespoons tequila (optional)

1 teaspoon dark palm sugar, or to taste

1 sprig mint, leaves only, to serve

Place the pawpaw, pineapple, lime juice, mineral water and
tequila into a blender or food processor and blend until smooth.
Stir in the sugar to taste. Pour into an airtight container and chill,
in the refrigerator, until ready to serve.

Pour into shot glasses and garnish with mint leaves and
the reserved pawpaw seeds. Serve immediately.

## COOLING REFRESHERS

Teas and herbs have been used by many generations for calming nerves, healing, aiding digestion, and for their reviving properties.

The following refreshing drinks are perfect to take along to a sporting day, a picnic at the beach or as a special reward at the end of a bushwalk. Fill up the thermos or pack the esky, or, if all you end up doing is pulling a few weeds out of the garden, pop into the kitchen and whip up something refreshing to enjoy as you sit back and admire the results of your hard work!

## Pineapple, cucumber and mint cooler

Makes about 600 ml (serves 2–3)
400 g pineapple flesh, cut into chunks
2 Lebanese cucumbers, cut into chunks
4 sprigs mint
crushed ice, to serve

Using an electric juicer, process the pineapple, cucumber and mint. Pour into glasses over crushed ice.

## Buttermilk cooler with frozen berries and lime

*This calcium-rich cooler will kick-start any breakfast party with taste and flair!*

**Makes about 700 ml (serves 2–3)**

400 g frozen berries (blackberries, strawberries, raspberries and/or boysenberries)

1 small lime, cut into thin wedges

200 ml chilled buttermilk

½ cup crushed ice

750 ml sparkling mineral water

In a 1-litre capacity jug, combine the berries, lime wedges, buttermilk and crushed ice. Top up with mineral water. Pour into glasses and serve.

## Champagne watermelon, ginger and lime refresher

*Champagne watermelons are a lovely pale yellow and make an attractive, sunny start to a brunch.*

Makes about 300 ml (serves 1–2)
400 g seedless Champagne watermelon flesh, cut into chunks
1 large (4 cm) knob fresh ginger, peeled
1 wedge lime, peeled
crushed ice, to serve

Using an electric juicer, process the watermelon, ginger and lime. Pour into glasses over crushed ice.

## Lychee, pineapple and mint cooler

*This lovely drink is refreshing and not too sweet, and can be frozen into a delicious slush. A little white rum would be a nice addition.*

Makes about 500 ml (serves 10 shots)

10 lychees, peeled and de-stoned

100 g pineapple flesh, peeled and cut into chunks

300 ml freshly brewed mint tea, cooled

2 tablespoons freshly squeezed lime juice

crushed ice, to serve

Place the lychees, pineapple, tea and lime juice into a blender or food processor and blend. Pour into shot glasses over crushed ice.

## Fennel, ginger, lemon and mint refresher

*A good digestive drink, serve this refresher after lunch or dinner.*

Makes about 500 ml (serves 2)
2 tablespoons fennel seeds, crushed
1 small (2 cm) knob fresh ginger, peeled and crushed
1 x 2 cm strip lemon rind
500 ml boiling water
1 sprig mint, leaves only, finely chopped
crushed ice, to serve

Crush the fennel seeds and ginger lightly together using a mortar and pestle. Place the fennel seeds, ginger and lemon rind into a coffee plunger, then pour in the boiling water.

Allow to cool completely, then depress the coffee plunger. Pour into a jug, stir in the mint leaves, then pour into glasses over crushed ice.

## Mint and tomato refresher

*This tomato and mint refresher has an unusual flavour. Serve in shot glasses with an oyster as a shooter! Alternatively, try it with a garnish of chopped basil leaves.*

Makes about 600 ml (serves 12 shots)
8 ripe tomatoes, cut into chunks
1 small wedge lime, peeled
300 ml freshly brewed mint tea, cooled
ground black pepper
pinch of sea salt
crushed ice, to serve

Using an electric juicer, process the tomato and lime. Stir in the tea and season well with pepper and sea salt. Pour into shot glasses over crushed ice and serve immediately.

## Iced lemongrass, lemon balm and mint tea

*How cool can cool be? Try lemongrass, mint, lime and a little honey over crushed ice!*

**Makes about 500 ml (serves 2)**
1–2 tablespoons lemongrass tea leaves
¼ cup lemon balm leaves
½–1 tablespoon honey
500 ml boiling water
juice of 1 lime
6 mint leaves, gently crushed and roughly torn
crushed ice, to serve

Place the lemongrass tea, lemon balm leaves and honey in a coffee plunger and pour over the boiling water.

Allow to cool completely, then depress the coffee plunger. Pour into a jug, then stir in the lime juice and mint leaves. Pour into glasses over crushed ice.

# Lime refresher with ginger

*Help take the heat out of the day with a glass of chilled tea combined with lime and ginger and then topped up with sparkling mineral water.*

**Makes about 650 ml (serves 2–3)**

½ large lime, thinly sliced

1 small (2 cm) knob fresh ginger, peeled and bruised, then grated

600 ml freshly brewed Indian tea, cooled

juice from ½ lime

2–3 tablespoons dark honey, or to taste

1–2 cups crushed ice

200 ml sparkling mineral water

Add the lime and ginger to the tea. Stir in the lime juice and add honey to taste. Pour into a jug, add the crushed ice and top with mineral water. Serve in tall glasses.

## Apple and citrus with 'the Earl' refresher

*A drink to serve when the* boules *or croquet set is dusted off!*

**Makes about 500 ml (serves 2)**
3 apples, quartered and cored
1 small wedge lemon, peeled (but with some white pith remaining)
¼ orange, peeled (but with some white pith remaining)
250 ml freshly brewed strong Earl Grey tea, chilled
½ lemon, thinly sliced
½ orange thinly sliced
6 sprigs mint
1 cup crushed ice

Using an electric juicer, process the apple, lemon wedge and
¼ orange. Strain the tea and stir into the juice. Add the orange
and lemon slices, the mint and the crushed ice. Pour into a serving
jug and serve immediately.

## Spicy lemons and ginger

*A refreshing, spicy juice – a taste of tea with the Raj!*

Makes about 500 ml (serves 2)

2 tablespoons lemon balm tea leaves

2 tablespoons dark honey or dark palm sugar

1 tablespoon grated fresh ginger

1 stick cinnamon

4 whole cloves

500 ml boiling water

juice of 1 large lemon

½ cup crushed ice

lemon balm leaves, to serve

Place the lemon balm tea, honey, ginger, cinnamon and cloves into a coffee plunger, then pour over the boiling water.

Allow to cool completely, then chill in the refrigerator. To serve, pour the lemon juice into a jug, then strain in the tea. Add the crushed ice and pour into glasses decorated with lemon balm leaves.

# FRUIT SLUSHES

Ice-cool and delicious, fruit slushes are a great way to end a meal. Serve in little rice bowls with teaspoons, or in martini glasses; the more imaginative you are with the serving, the more impressive a fruit slush will be at the end of a special dinner.

## Green tea and ice slush

*For this recipe, use green tea leaves, if available, rather than a tea bag. The flavour will be much nicer.*

**Makes about 600 ml (serves 3–4)**
300 ml freshly brewed green tea
2 tablespoons freshly squeezed lemon juice
300 ml frozen vanilla yoghurt

Allow the tea to steep and, when completely cool, strain and place in the refrigerator to chill.

Stir the lemon juice into the tea, then pour into a blender or food processor. Add the frozen yoghurt and blend until combined. Pour into small glasses and serve with a spoon.

## Cranberry, blackberry and yoghurt slush

*This delicious drink can be made ahead of time and kept in the fridge until ready to serve.*

**Makes about 600 ml (serves 2–3)**

250 ml cranberry juice

300 g frozen blackberries

250 ml plain yoghurt

3 tablespoons palm sugar

Place all the ingredients into a blender or food processor and blend until smooth. Spoon into long glasses and serve immediately.

## Coconut, guava, banana and lychee slush

*Guavas are only in season for a short period of time, so instead of using fresh guava juice look for guava nectar, available year round from Asian supermarkets and some grocery stores.*

Makes about 600 ml (serves 2–3)
125 ml light coconut milk
250 ml frozen guava nectar, cut into chunks
1 frozen banana, peeled and cut into chunks
8 lychees, peeled, de-stoned and chopped
1 lime, to serve

Place the coconut milk, guava nectar and banana in a blender or food processor and blend until thick and smooth. Stir in the lychees, then spoon into tall glasses and add a squeeze of lime to each. Serve immediately.

## Guava, strawberry and yoghurt slush

**Makes about 600 ml (serves 2–3)**
400 ml frozen guava nectar, cut into chunks
200 ml vanilla yoghurt
8 strawberries, hulled and chopped
1 peach, de-stoned and cut into small chunks

Place the guava nectar and yoghurt in a blender or food processor and blend until smooth. Stir in the strawberries and peach. Spoon into long glasses and serve immediately.

## Watermelon and lychee slush

*Add a drizzle of tequila or vodka to this recipe to make it very grown-up!*

**Makes about 600 ml (serves 12 shots)**
500 g seedless watermelon flesh, cut into chunks
10 lychees, peeled and de-stoned
2 tablespoons freshly squeezed lime juice
3 tablespoons palm sugar

Place all the ingredients into a blender or food processor and blend until smooth. Pour into a shallow metal baking tray and transfer to the freezer for 2–3 hours, stirring with a fork every half hour or so during freezing to prevent the liquid setting hard. Spoon into shot glasses and serve immediately.

# Approximate Measurements

The following table contains useful approximate measurements for some of the more common ingredients in the book.

apple (medium) = 110 g

apricot (small) = 70 g

avocado (medium) = 225 g

banana (medium) = 225 g

berries (1 punnet) = 225–250 g

cabbage (half) = 800 g

capsicum (medium) = 125 g

carrot (medium) = 110 g

celery (1 stalk) = 80 g

cherries (1 cup) = 140 g

cucumber (Lebanese) = 130 g

english spinach (1 bunch, stalks removed) = 260 g

grapefruit (medium) = 130 ml juice

grapes (1 cup) = 130 g

fennel (medium) = 300 g

figs (1 fresh) = 30 g

lemon (medium) = 40 ml juice, 1 tablespoon grated zest

lettuce (head) = 350 g

lime (medium) = 20 ml juice, 1 teaspoon grated zest

mango (medium) = 400 g

melon (medium) = 1.5 kg

nectarine (medium) = 160 g

orange (medium) = 125 ml juice, 2 tablespoons grated zest

parsley (1 bunch) = 110 g

pawpaw (medium) = 400 g

peach (medium) = 110 g

pear (medium) = 100 g

pineapple (medium) = 1.2 kg

plum (small) = 50 g

tomato (medium) = 100 g

watercress (1 bunch) = 350 g

watermelon (medium) = 5–6 kg

zucchini (medium) = 100 g

# Index